PIANO • VOCAL • GUITAR

GOLDEN HOUR
KACEY MUSGRAVES

T0088557

ISBN 978-1-5400-5213-1

Visit Hal Leonard Online at
www.halleonard.com

Contact us:
Hal Leonard
7777 West Bluemound Road
Milwaukee, WI 53213
Email: info@halleonard.com

In Europe, contact:
Hal Leonard Europe Limited
42 Wigmore Street
Marylebone, London, W1U 2RN
Email: info@halleonardeurope.com

In Australia, contact:
Hal Leonard Australia Pty. Ltd.
4 Lentara Court
Cheltenham, Victoria, 3192 Australia
Email: info@halleonard.com.au

SLOW BURN

Words and Music by KACEY MUSGRAVES,
IAN FITCHUK and DANIEL TASHIAN

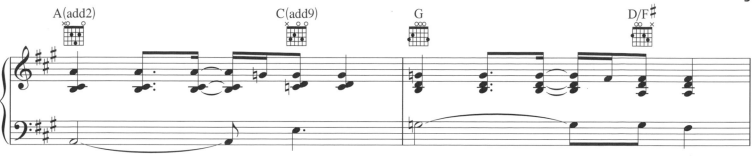

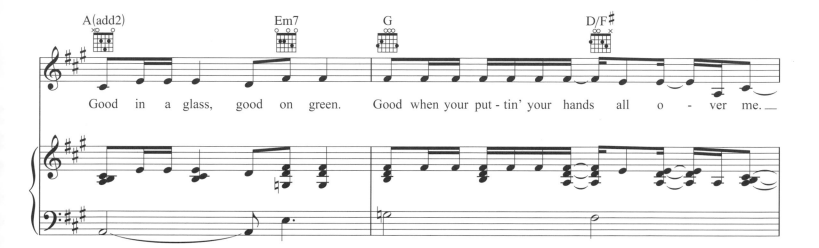

Good in a glass, good on green. Good when your put-tin' your hands all o - ver me.

I'm al - right _ with a slow burn. _____

Tak-in' my _ time, _ let the world turn. _____ I'm gon-na

do it my way, it-'ll be al - right if we burn it down and it takes all night. It's a

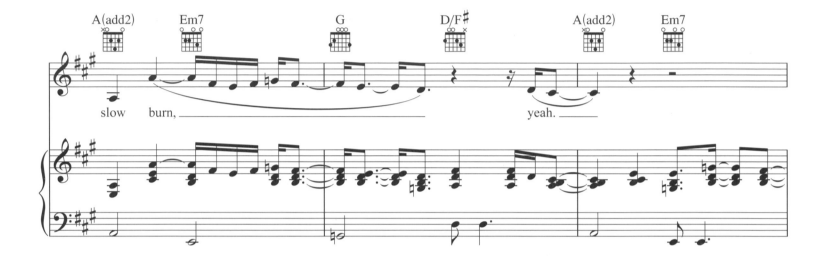

slow burn, _____ yeah. _____

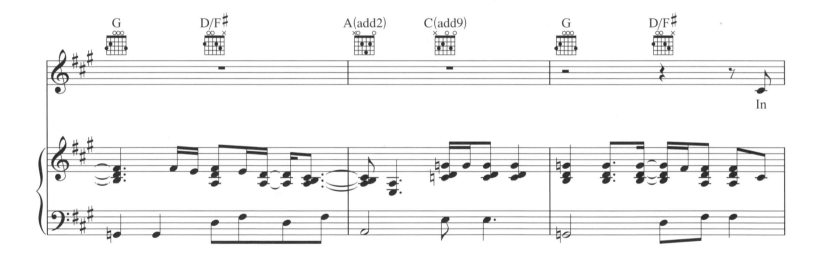

In

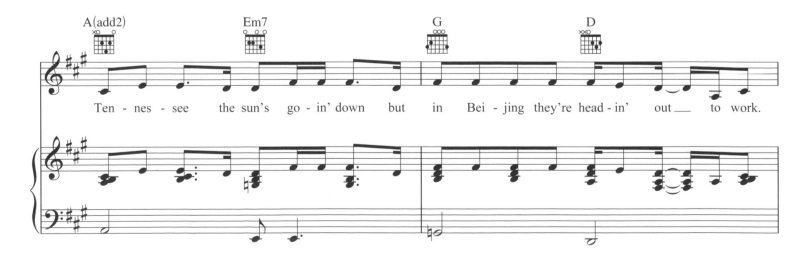

Ten - nes - see the sun's go - in' down but in Bei - jing they're head - in' out ___ to work.

You know the

bar down the street don't close for an hour. We should take a walk and look at all the flow-

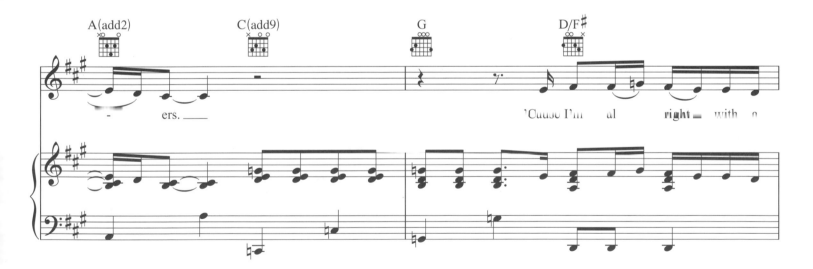

-ers. _____ 'Cause I'm al right _ with a

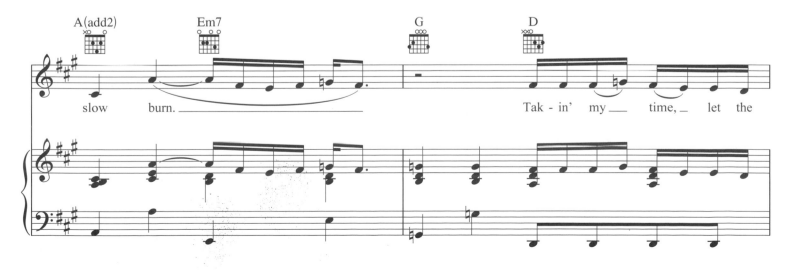

slow burn. _____ Tak-in' my _ time, _ let the

world turn. _____ I'm gon-na do it my way, it-'ll be al-right

if we burn it down and it take all night. It's a slow burn. _____

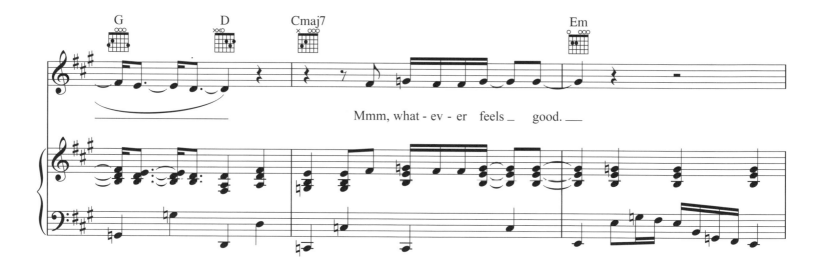

Mmm, what-ev-er feels_ good. __

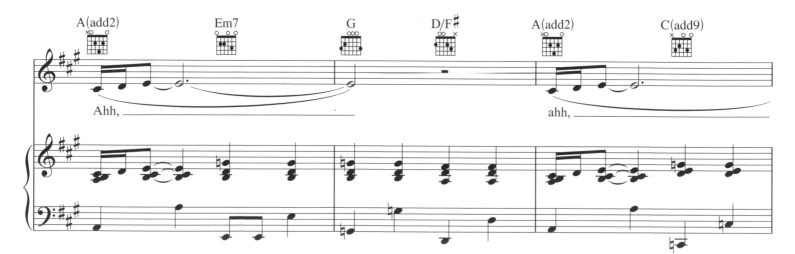

Ahh, _____ ahh, _____

ahh,

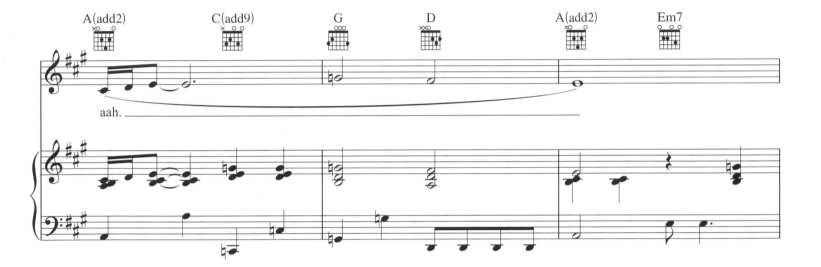

aah.

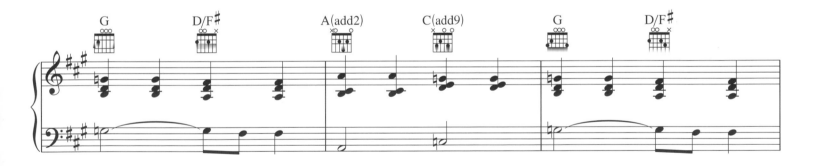

Old soul, wait-in' my turn. I know a few things but I still got a lot to learn.

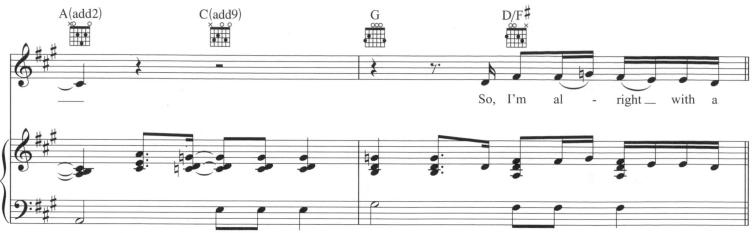

So, I'm al - right __ with a

slow   burn,
(Lead vocal ad lib. on repeat.)

slow   burn, _____

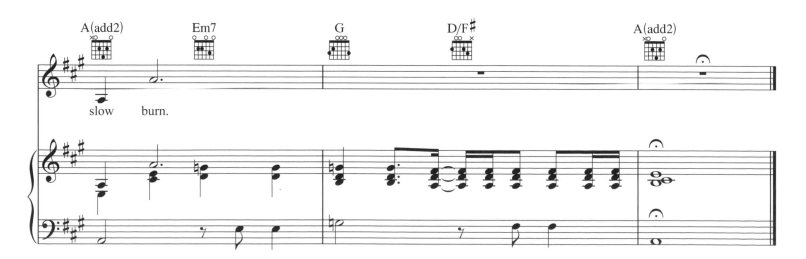

slow   burn.

LONELY WEEKEND

Words and Music by KACEY MUSGRAVES,
IAN FITCHUK and DANIEL TASHIAN

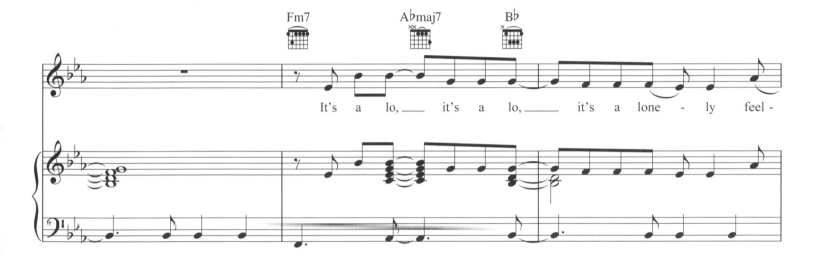

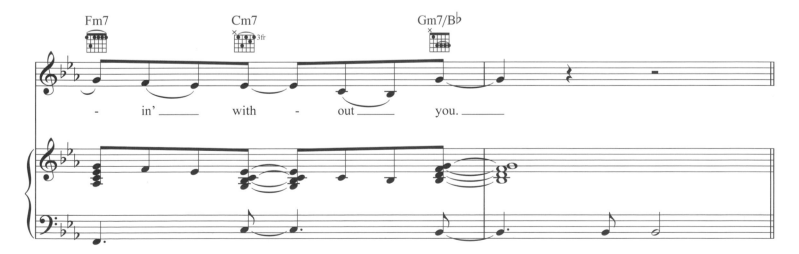

Mon - day I was gone and Tues - day you were work - in' late. ___
mil - lion things to do, but I have - n't done a sin - gle one. ___

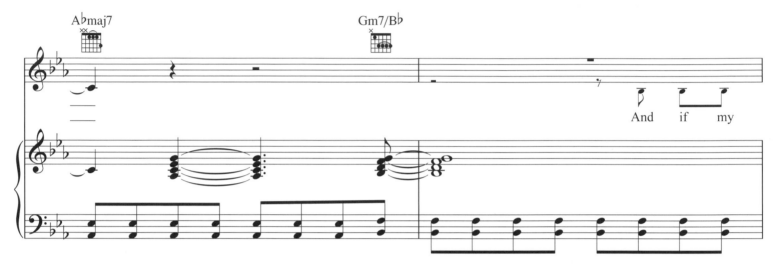

___ And if my

Wed - 'sday went to hell, then Thurs - day kind - a had to wait, ___
sis - ter lived in town, I know that we'd be do - in' some - thin' fun, ___

___ yeah. ___
___ mm. ___ I keep

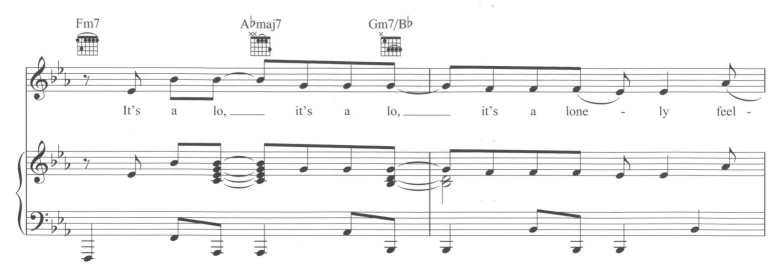

It's a lo,_____ it's a lo,_____ it's a lone - ly feel-

-in'_____ with - out_____ you._____ I guess

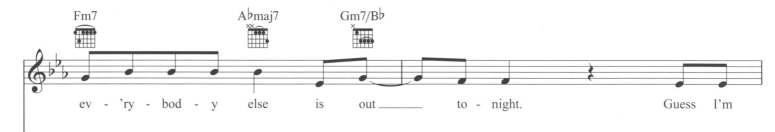

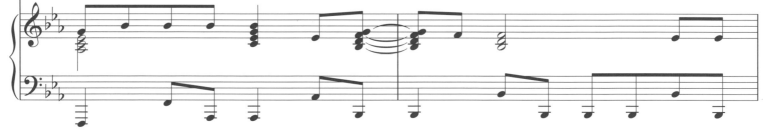

ev - 'ry - bod - y else is out_____ to - night. Guess I'm

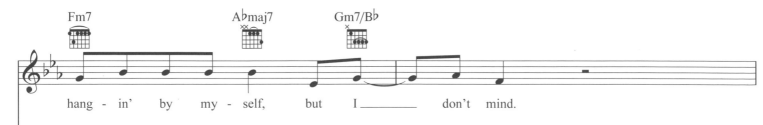

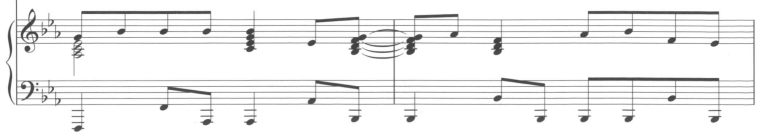

hang - in' by my - self, but I_____ don't mind.

it's al - right __ to be a - lone some - times, __

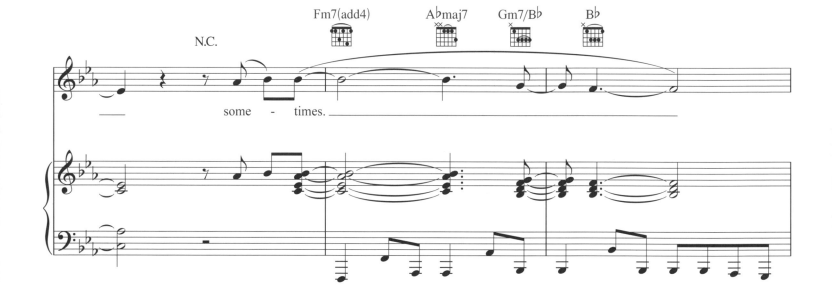

some - times. __

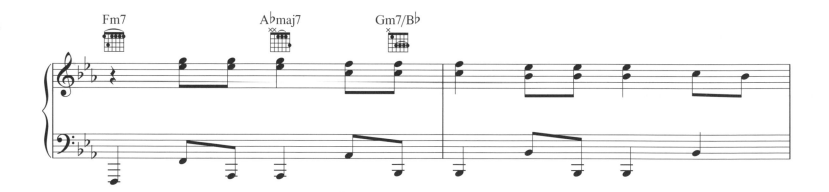

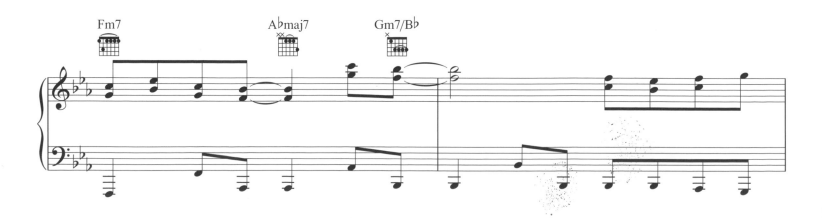

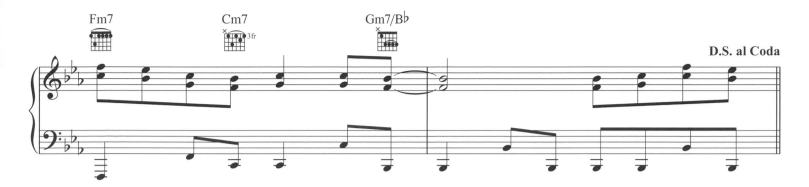

D.S. al Coda

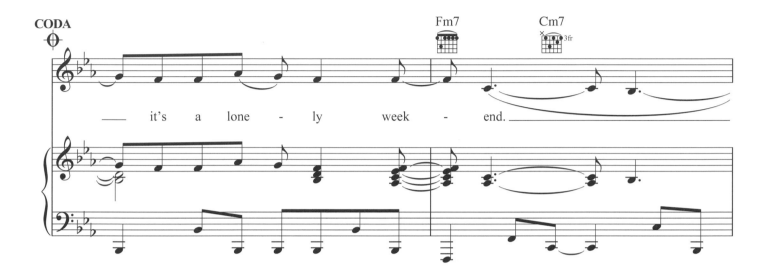

CODA

_____ it's a lone - ly week - end. _____

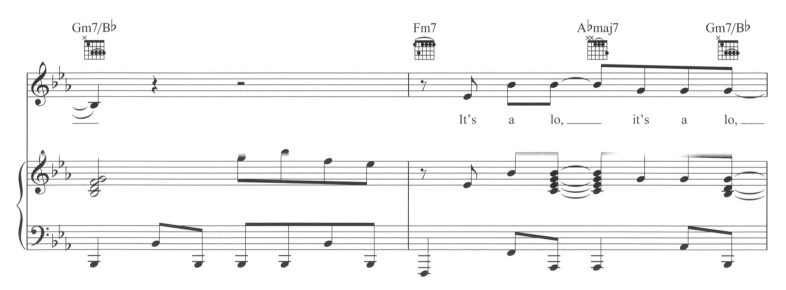

It's a lo, _____ it's a lo, _____

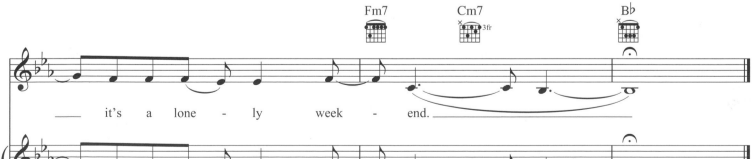

_____ it's a lone - ly week - end. _____

BUTTERFLIES

Words and Music by KACEY MUSGRAVES,
LUKE LAIRD and NATALIE HEMBY

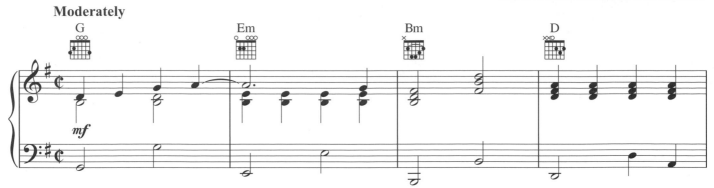

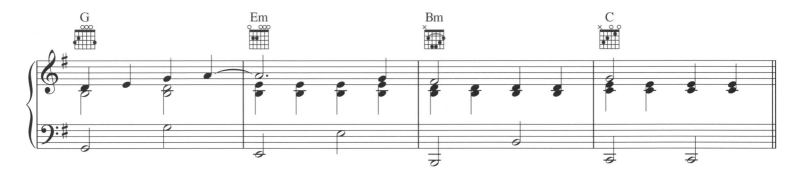

I was just coast-in', nev-er real-ly go-in' an-y-where.
Kiss full of col-or, makes me won-der where you've al-ways been.

Caught up in a web, I was get-tin' kind-a used to
I was hid-in' in ____ doubt till you brought me ____ out of my

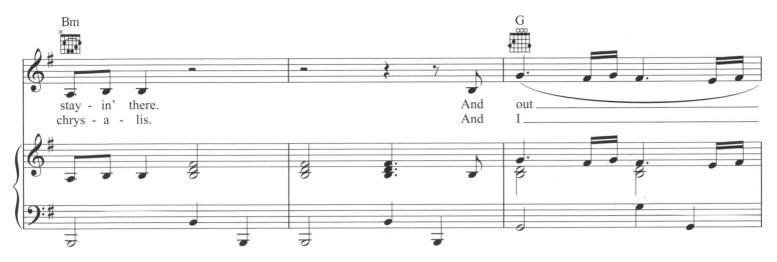

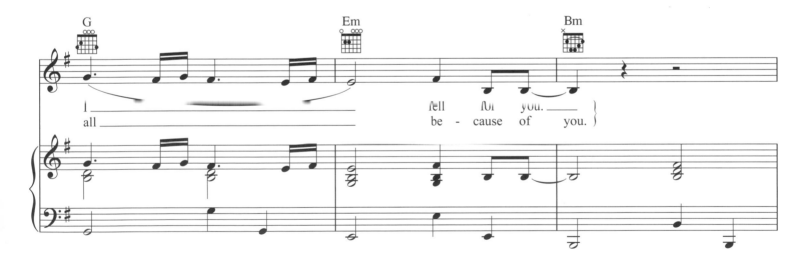

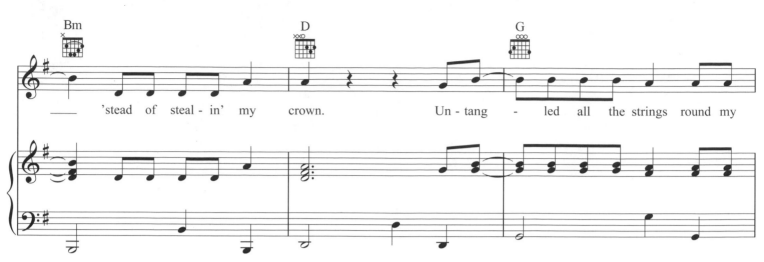

'stead of steal-in' my crown. Un-tang - led all the strings round my

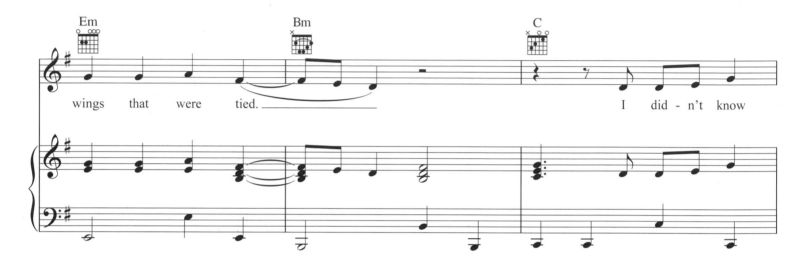

wings that were tied. _____ I did - n't know

him and I did - n't know me. Cloud nine ____ was al - ways out of reach. ____

Now I re - mem - ber what it feels like to ____ fly. ____

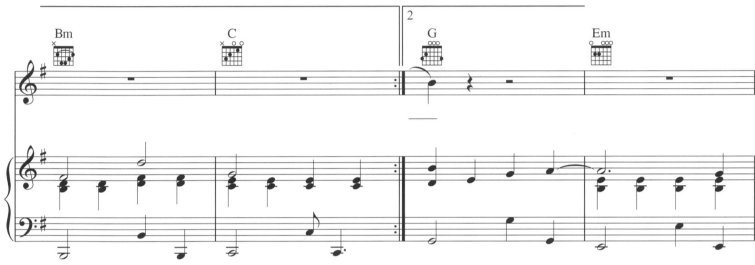

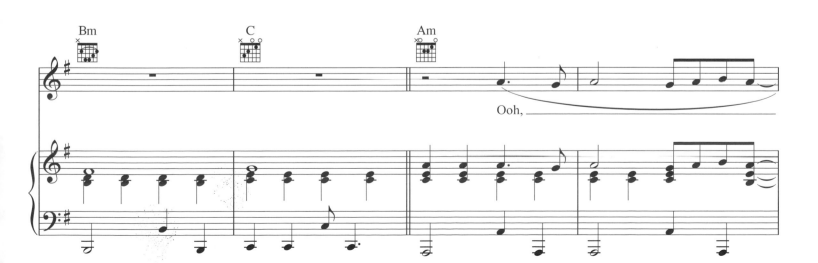

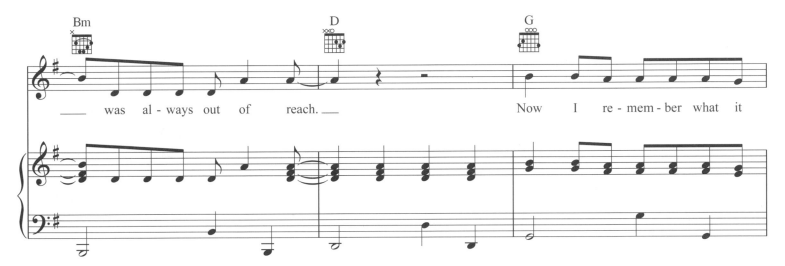

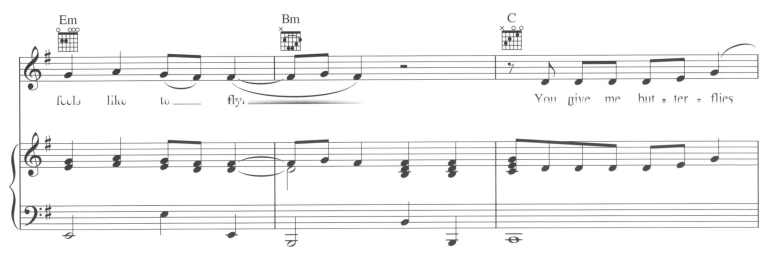

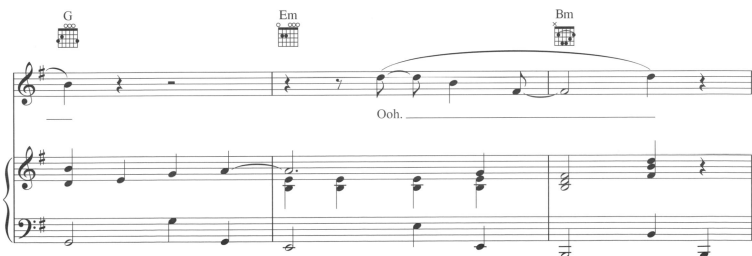

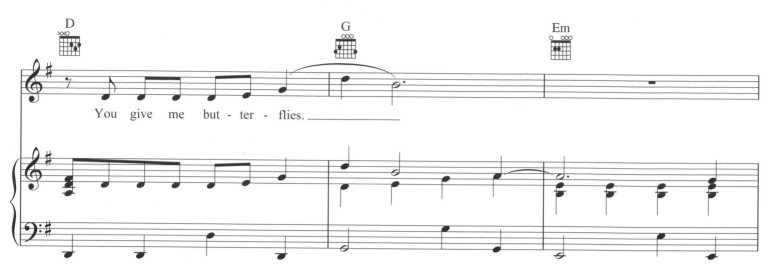

You give me but - ter - flies. _____

Mm. _____

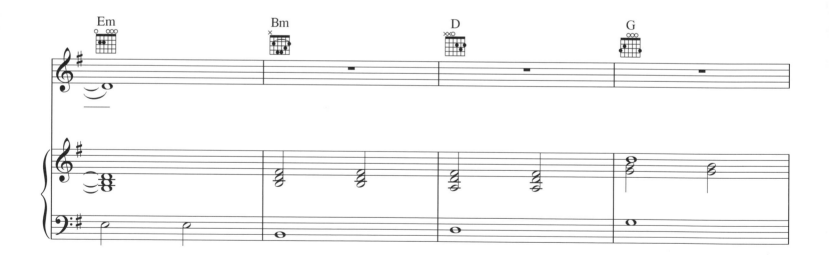

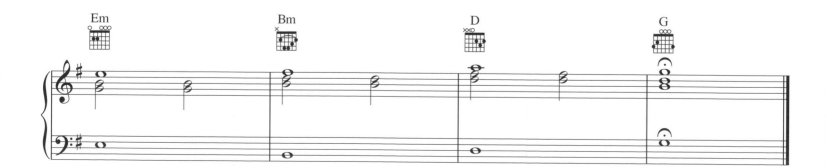

HIGH HORSE

Words and Music by KACEY MUSGRAVES,
TOMMY SCHLEITER and TRENT DABBS

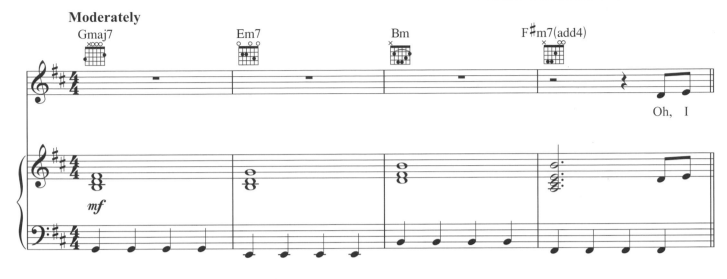

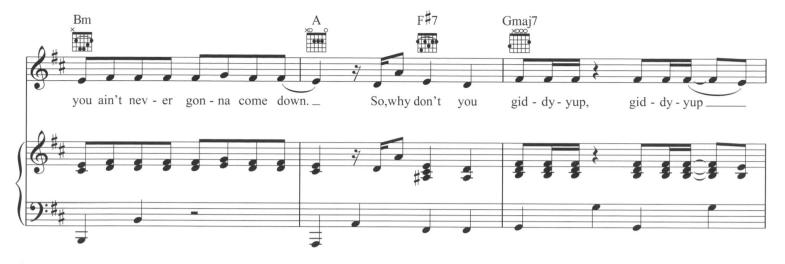

you ain't nev - er gon - na come down. ___ So, why don't you gid - dy - yup, gid - dy - yup ___

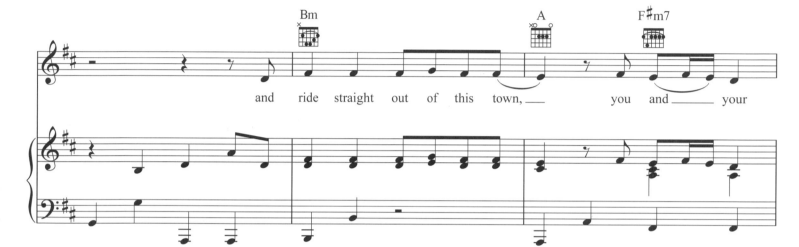

and ride straight out of this town, ___ you and ___ your

High ___ horse, ___

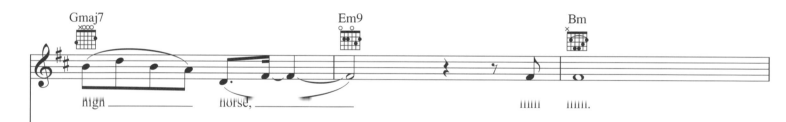

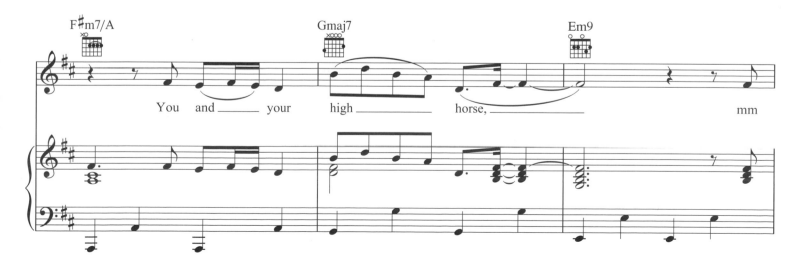

You and ___ your high ___ horse, ___ mm

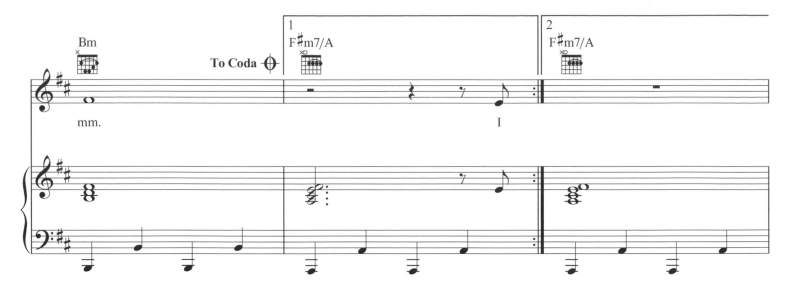

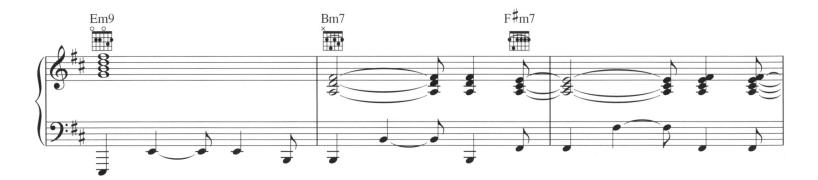

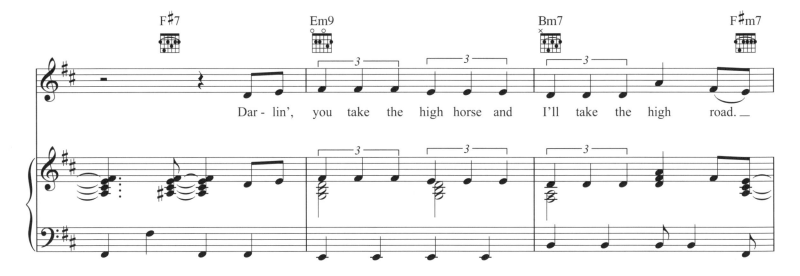

good rid - in' so - lo.   Yeah, I think we've

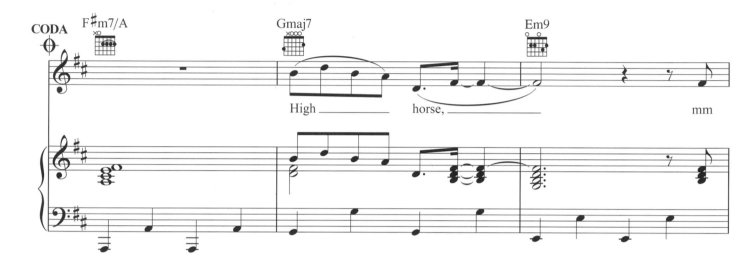

High _____ horse, _____   mm

mm.   You ain't nev - er gon - na come down.

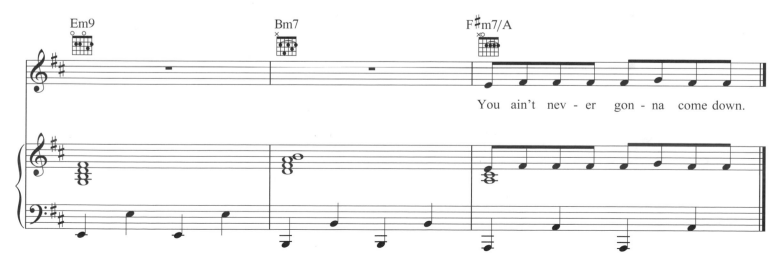

You ain't nev - er gon - na come down.

OH, WHAT A WORLD

Words and Music by KACEY MUSGRAVES,
IAN FITCHUK and DANIEL TASHIAN

Oh, what a world, _ I don't wan-na leave. _ There's all kinds of mag - ic, it's

hard to be - lieve. _ North - ern Lights in our skies.

Plants that grow and _ o - pen your mind. _ Things that swim

with a ne - on glow.   How we all got here, ___ no - bod - y knows.

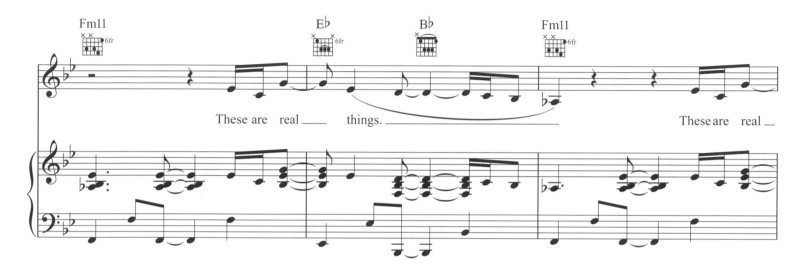

These are real ___ things. ___   These are real ___

things. Oh what a world,   don't wan - na leave, ___   All kinds of mag -

- ic all a - round us, it's hard to be - lieve. Thank God it's not ___ too good to be ___ true. ___

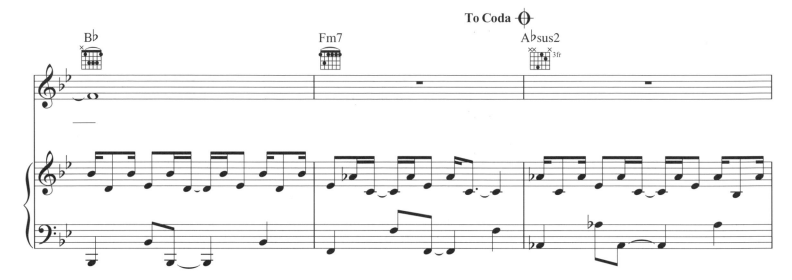

but it does - n't mat - ter 'cause you're here right now and I know what I feel.

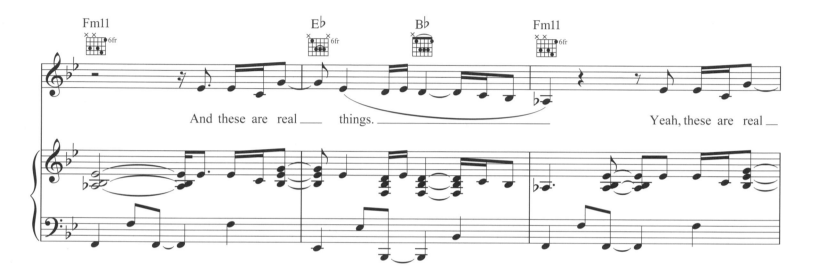

And these are real ___ things. ___ Yeah, these are real ___

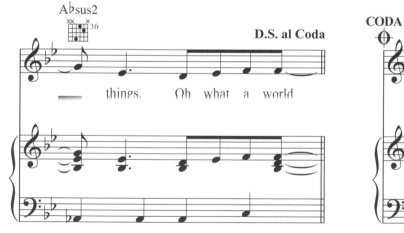

___ things. Oh what a world

Oh, ___

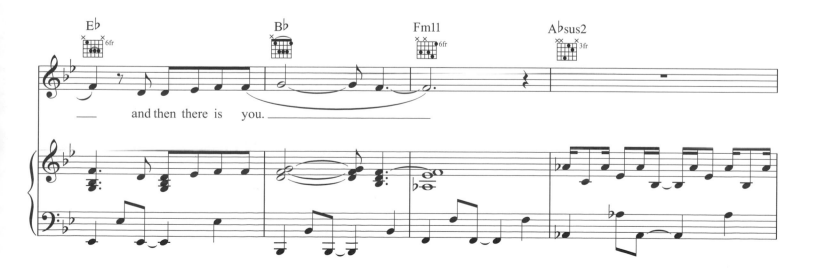

___ and then there is you. ___

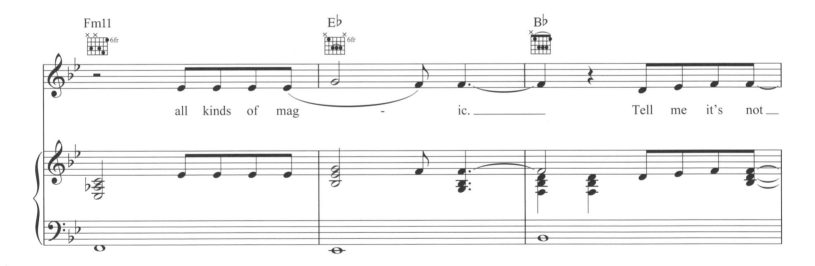

MOTHER

Words and Music by KACEY MUSGRAVES,
IAN FITCHUK and DANIEL TASHIAN

Slowly, with feeling

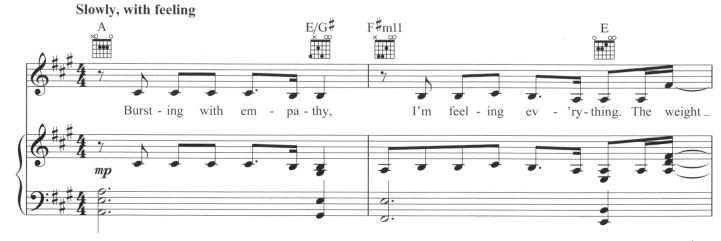

Burst-ing with em-pa-thy, I'm feel-ing ev-'ry-thing. The weight

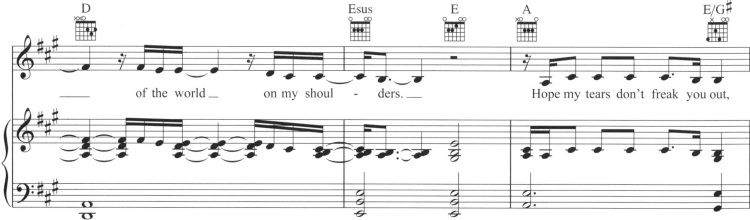

of the world on my shoul - ders. Hope my tears don't freak you out,

they're just kind-a com-in' out. It's the mus - ic in me and all of the col-

- ors. Wish we did-n't live, wish we did-n't live so far

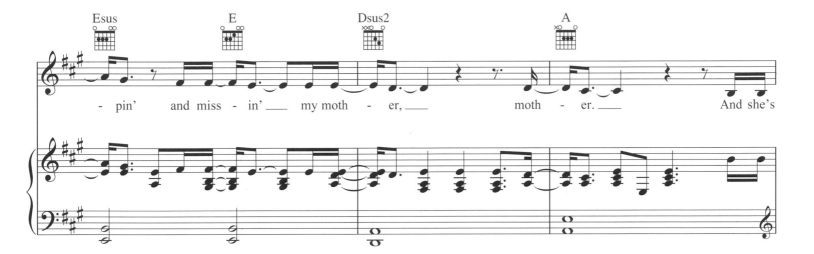

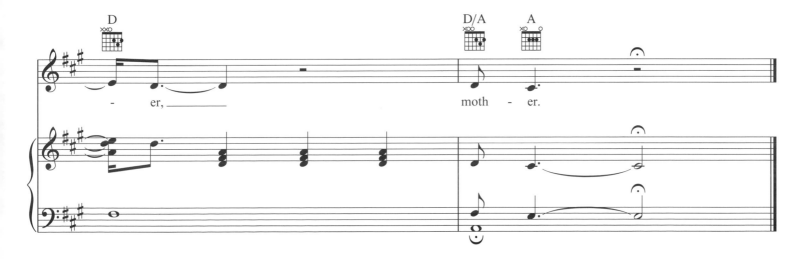

LOVE IS A WILD THING

Words and Music by KACEY MUSGRAVES,
IAN FITCHUK and DANIEL TASHIAN

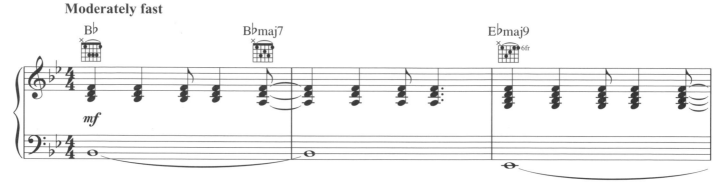

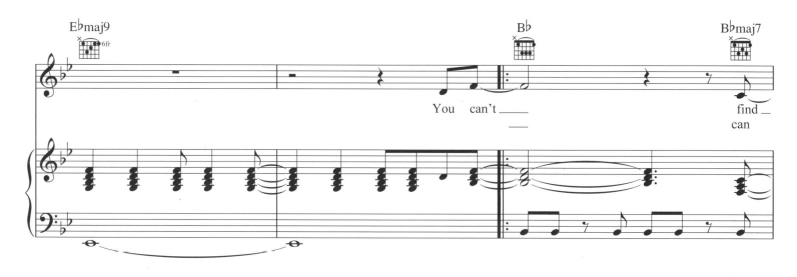

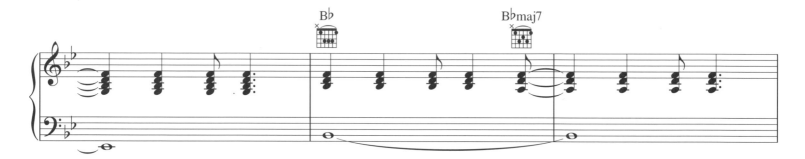

to hide ___ it, it's gon - na shine e - ven more. ___
can hear ___ it in the words com - in' off your lips. ___

E - ven if ___ you lose ___ it, it ___ will
E - ven if ___ you lose ___ me, I ___ will

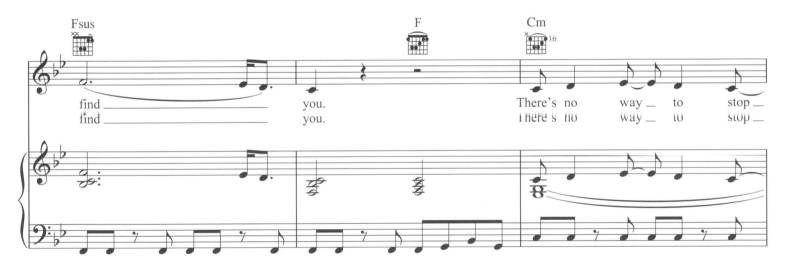

find _____ you.
find _____ you.

There's no way ___ to stop ___
There's no way ___ to stop ___

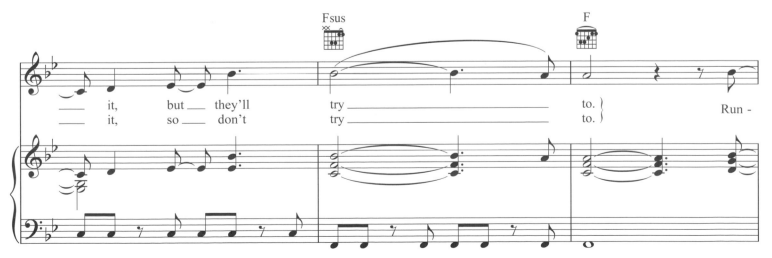

___ it, but ___ they'll try _____ to. }
___ it, so ___ don't try _____ to. }

Run -

-nin' like a riv-er, try'n' __ to find the o-cean, flow-ers in the con-crete. __

Climb-in' o-ver fenc-es, bloom-in' in the shad-ows,

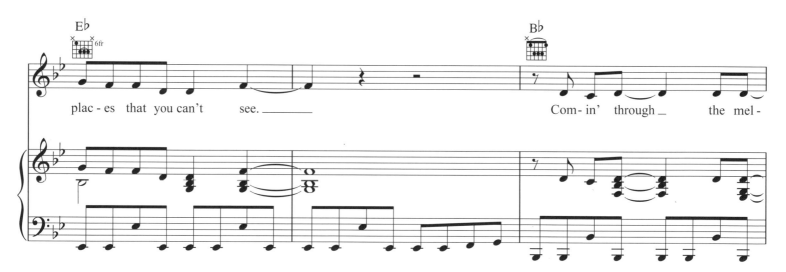

plac-es that you can't see. __ Com-in' through __ the mel-

-o-dy when the night __ bird __ sings, __

love is a wild _____ thing, _____

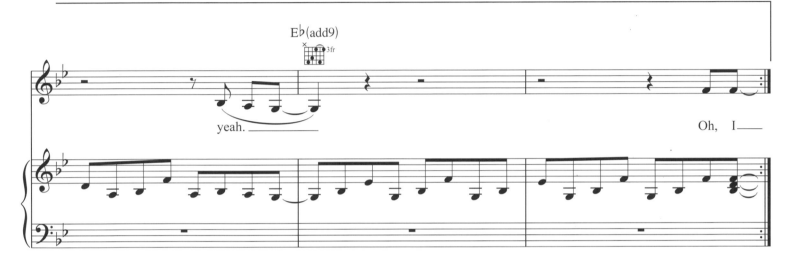

yeah. _____

Oh, I _____

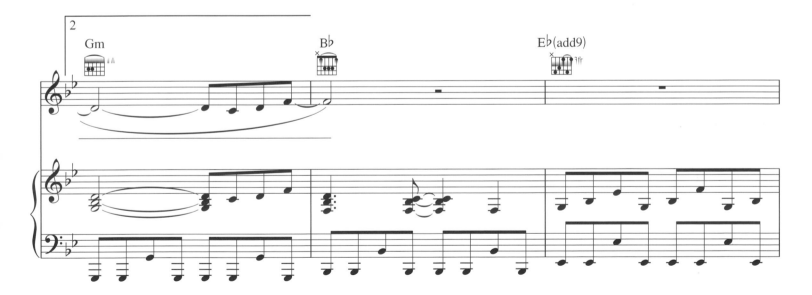

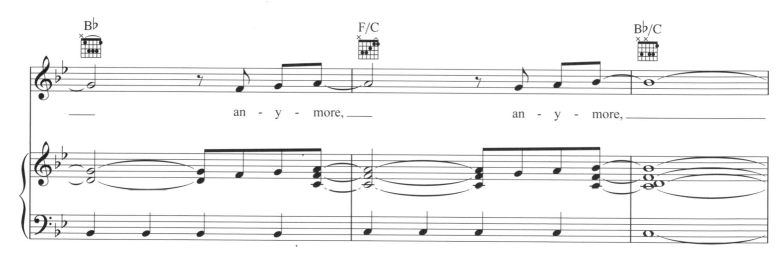

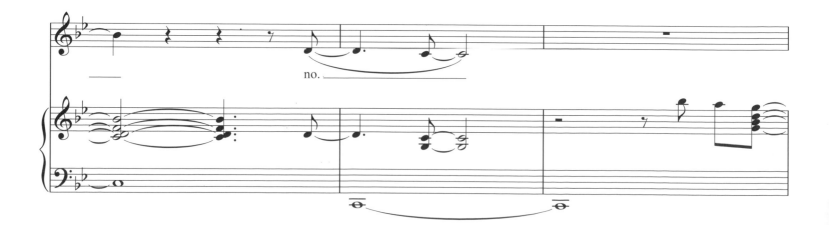

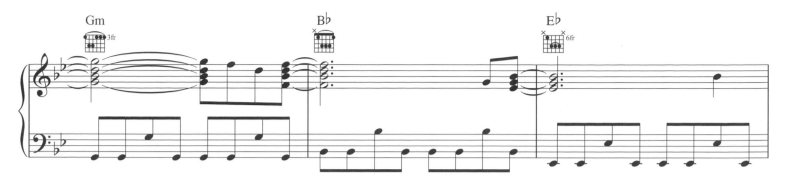

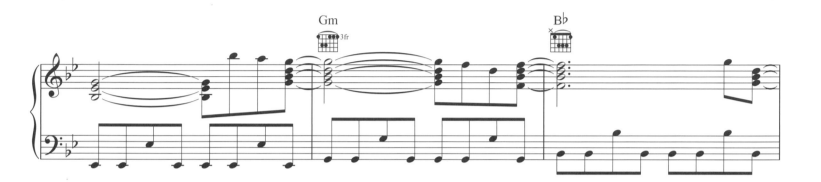

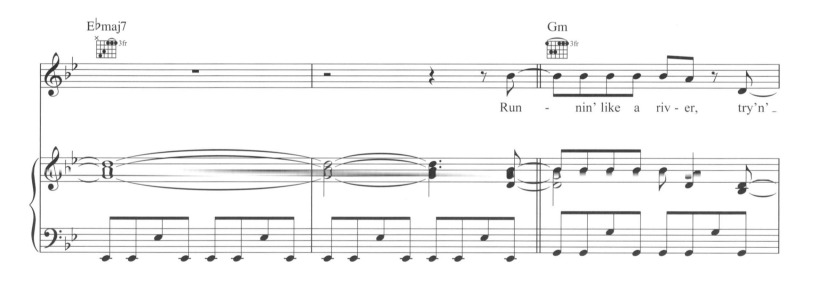

Run - nin' like a riv - er, try'n'

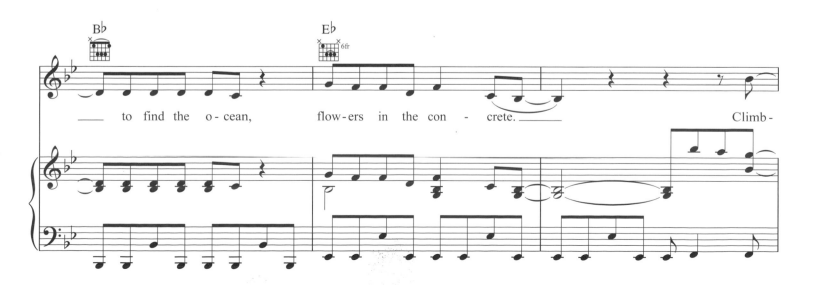

___ to find the o - cean, flow-ers in the con - crete. ___ Climb-

-in' o- ver fenc- es, bloom - in' in the shad- ows, plac- es that you can't see.____

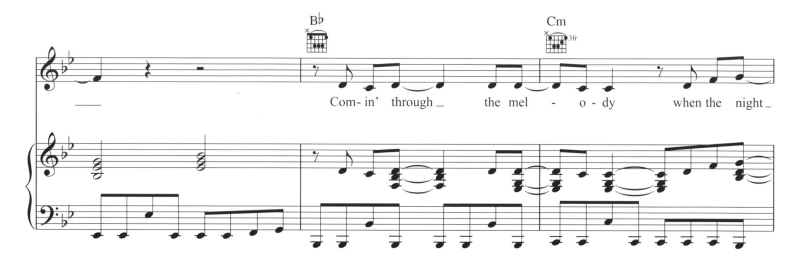

____ Com- in' through _ the mel - o- dy when the night _

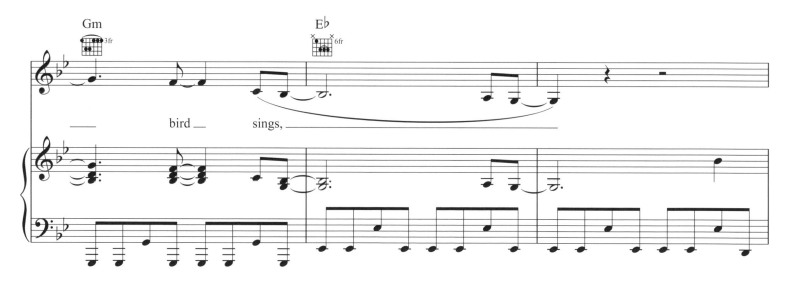

____ bird _ sings, _____

love is a wild _____ thing. ____

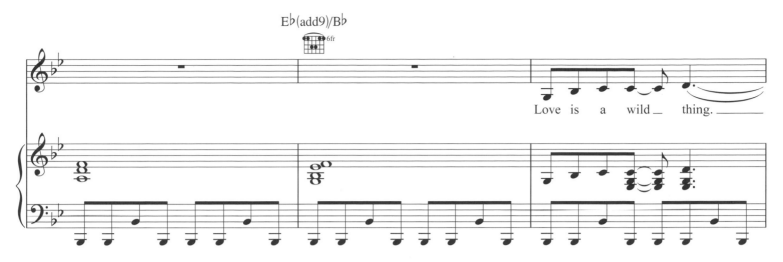

Love is a wild thing.

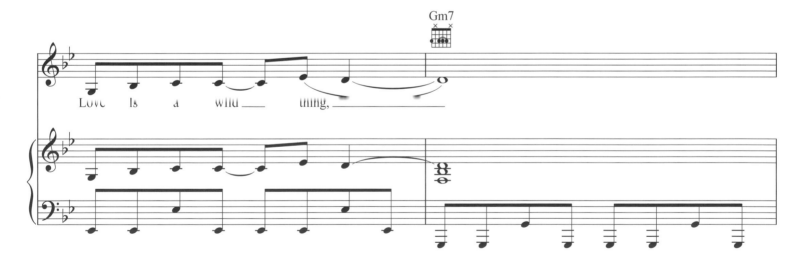

Love is a wild thing,

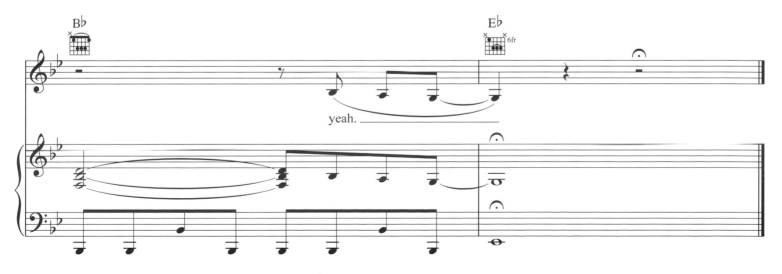

yeah.

SPACE COWBOY

Words and Music by KACEY MUSGRAVES,
LUKE LAIRD and SHANE McANALLY

Moderate Ballad

You look out the win-dow while I look at
Af-ter the gold rush, there ain't no rea-son to stay.

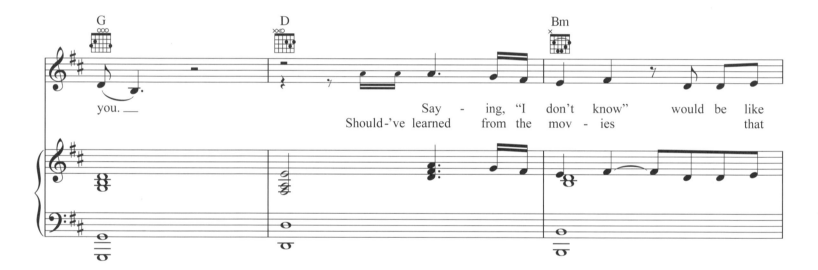

you. ___
Should-'ve learned from the mov-ies

Say - ing, "I don't know" would be like
that

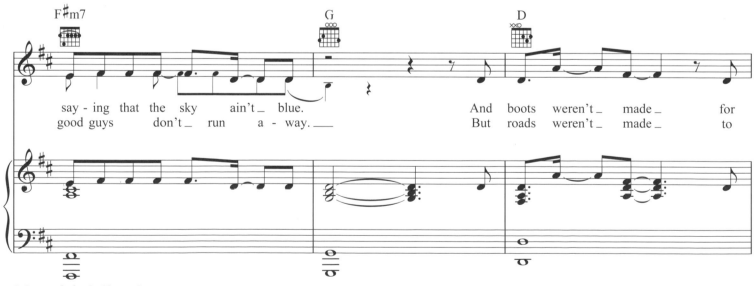

say-ing that the sky ain't_ blue.
good guys don't_ run a - way. ___

And boots weren't_ made_ for
But roads weren't_ made_ to

* Recorded a half step lower

sit - ting by ___ the door, ___ since you don't want to stay an - y - more. ___)
not ___ go ___ down ___ and there ain't room for both of us in this town. ___) You can have your

space, cow - boy. I ain't gon - na fence you in. ___

___ Go on, ride a - way In your Sil - ver - a - do,

guess I'll see you round a - gain. ___ I know my ___ place ___

and it ain't with __ you, __ well, sun - sets fade __ and love __ does too. __

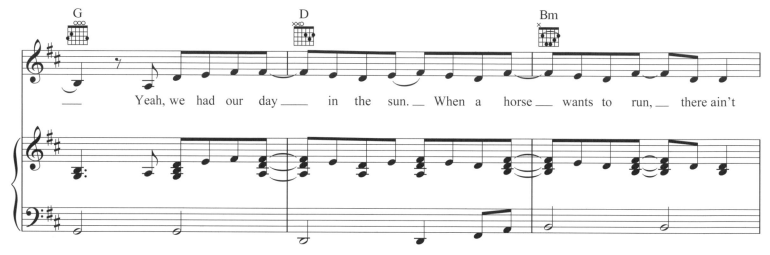

__ Yeah, we had our day __ in the sun. __ When a horse __ wants to run, __ there ain't

no sense in clos - ing the gate. ___ You can have your _ space, __

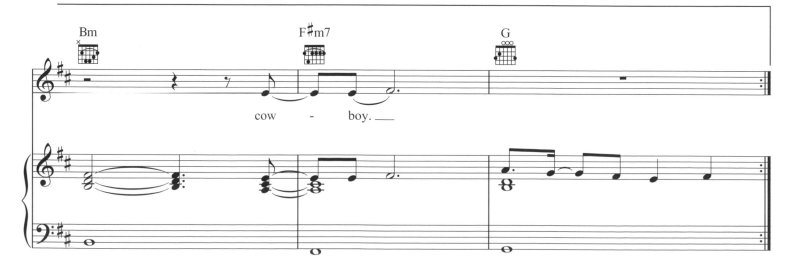

cow - boy. __

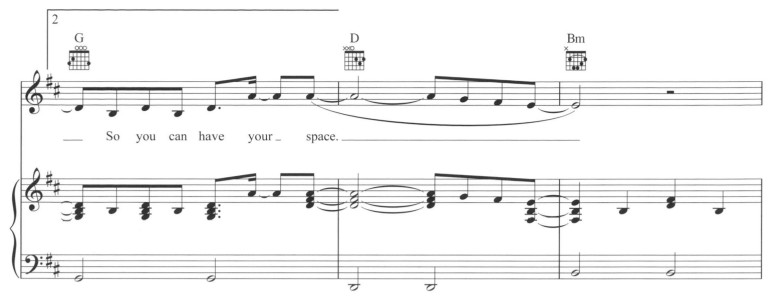

So you can have your space.

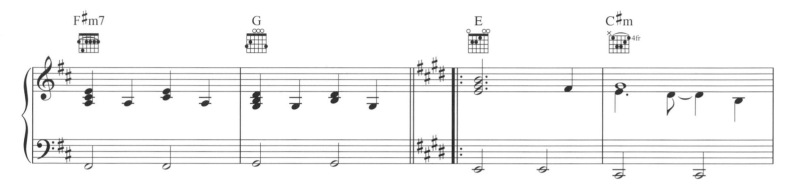

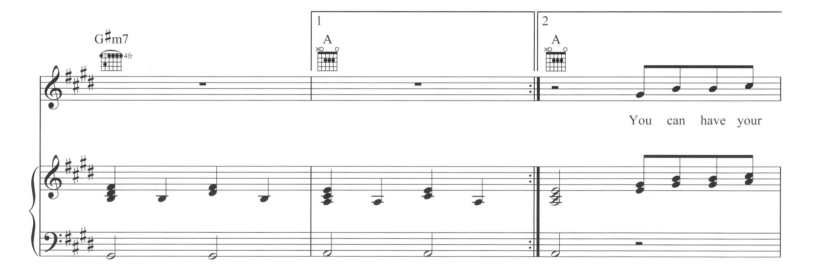

You can have your

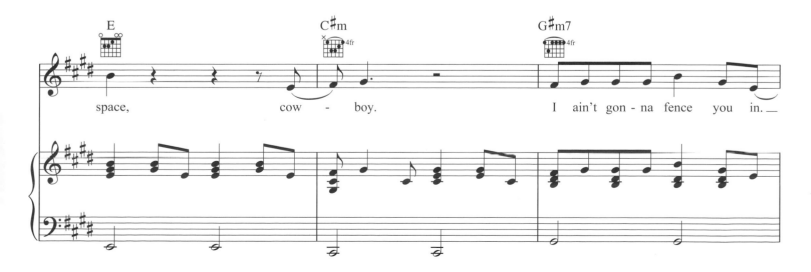

space, cow - boy. I ain't gon - na fence you in.

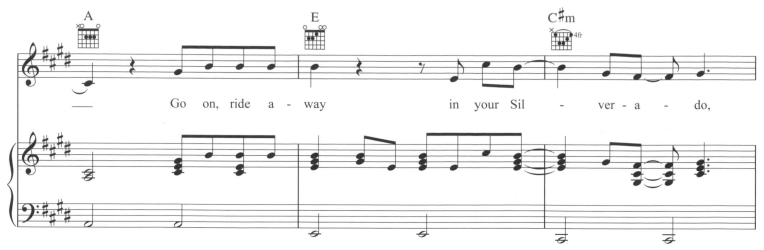

Go on, ride a - way in your Sil - ver - a - do,

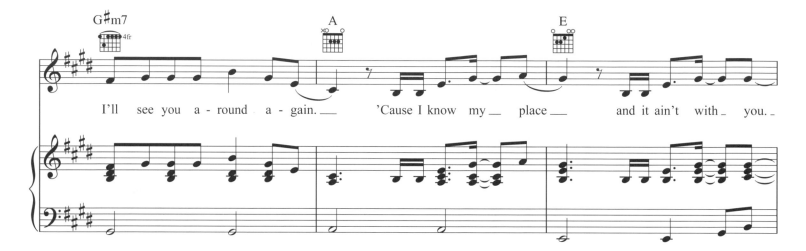

I'll see you a - round a - gain. ___ 'Cause I know my ___ place ___ and it ain't with ___ you. ___

___ Sun - sets fade ___ and love ___ does too. ___ Though we had our day ___

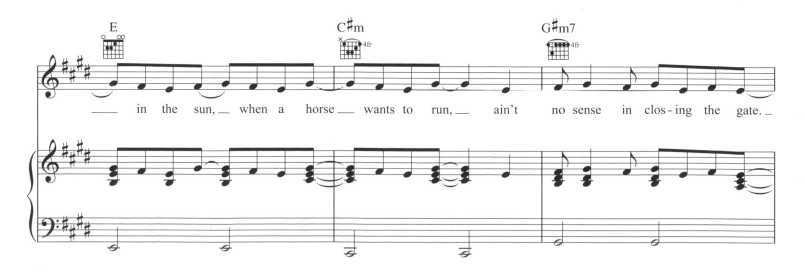

___ in the sun, ___ when a horse ___ wants to run, ___ ain't no sense in clos - ing the gate. ___

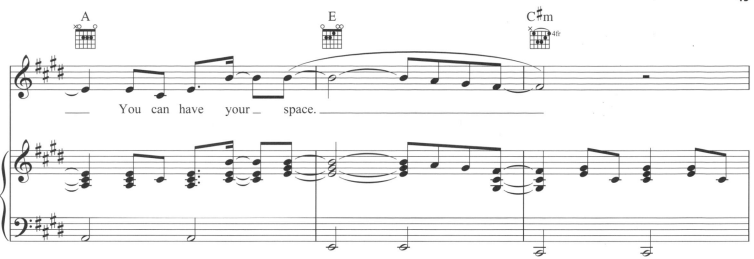

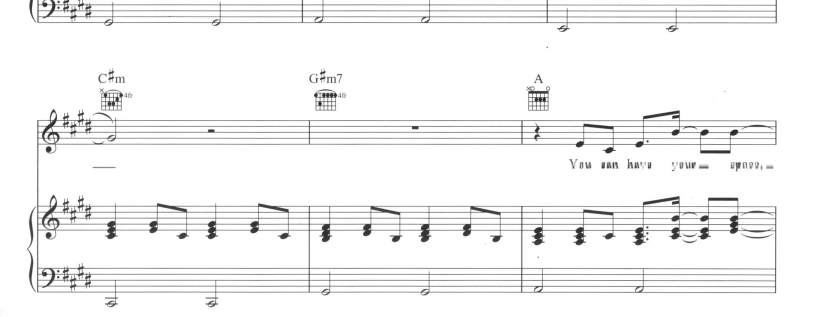

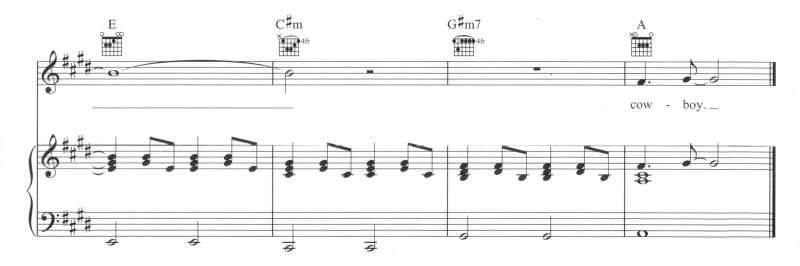

HAPPY & SAD

Words and Music by KACEY MUSGRAVES,
IAN FITCHUK and DANIEL TASHIAN

Moderately

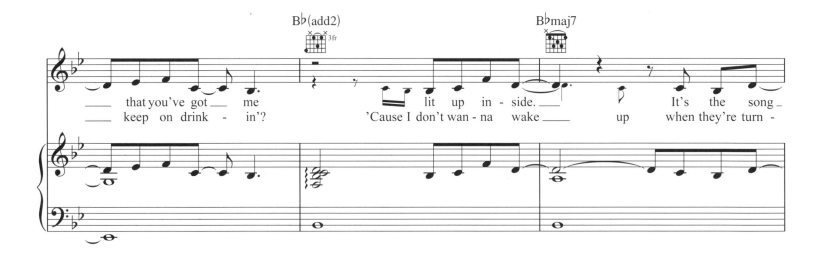

It's nev-er felt so right. }
'cause it feels so right. }
And

I'm the kind of per-son who starts get-tin' kind-a ner-vous when I'm hav-in' the time__ of my life.__

Is there a word__ for the way____ that I'm feel-in' to-night?__

Hap-py and sad__ at the same__ time. You got me smil-

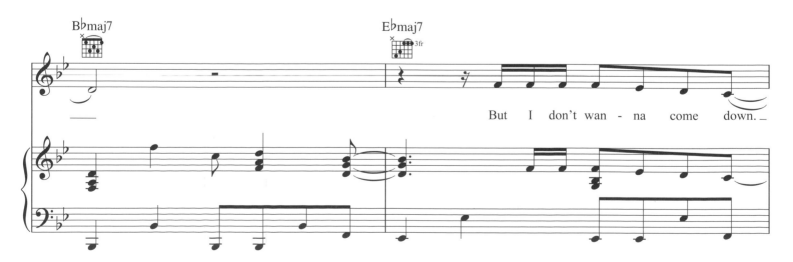

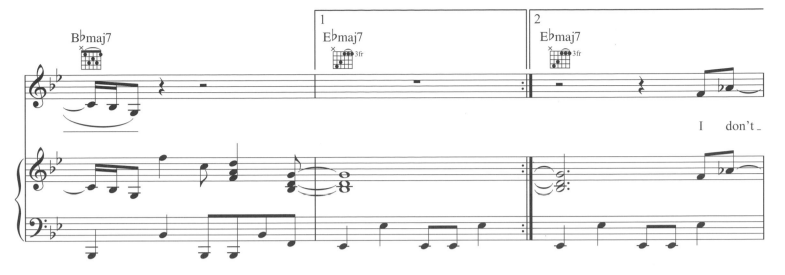

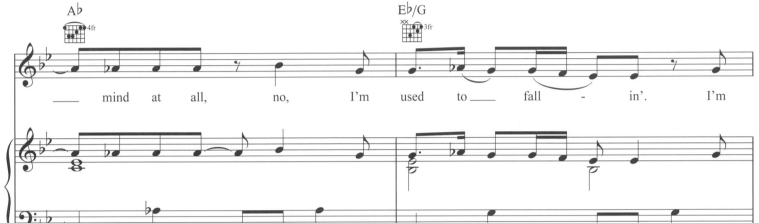

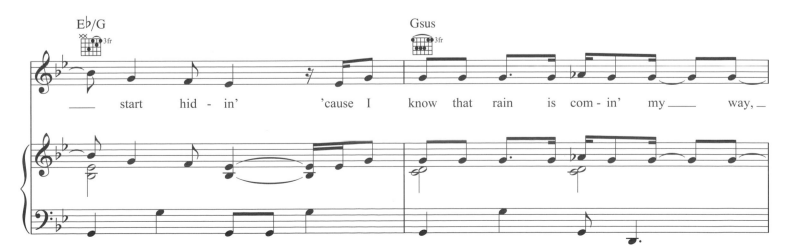

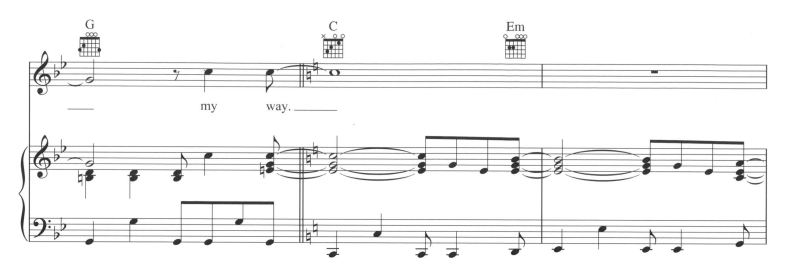

my way. _____

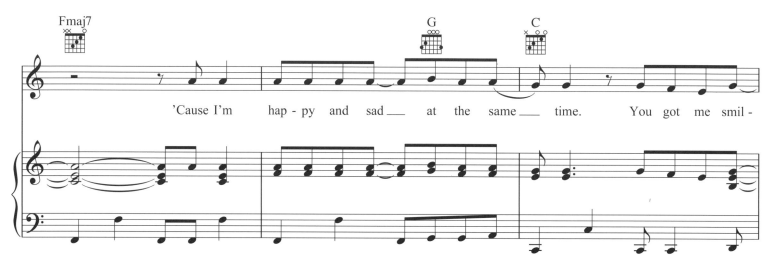

'Cause I'm hap - py and sad ___ at the same ___ time. You got me smil -

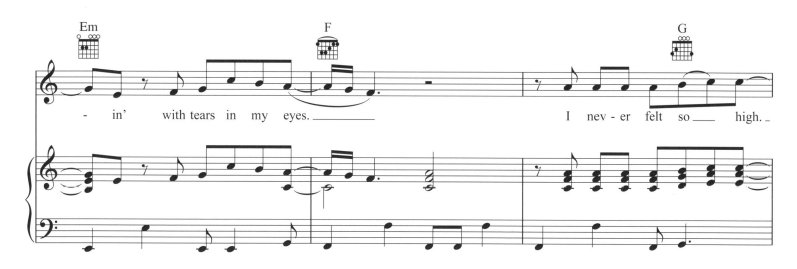

- in' with tears in my eyes. _____ I nev - er felt so ___ high. ___

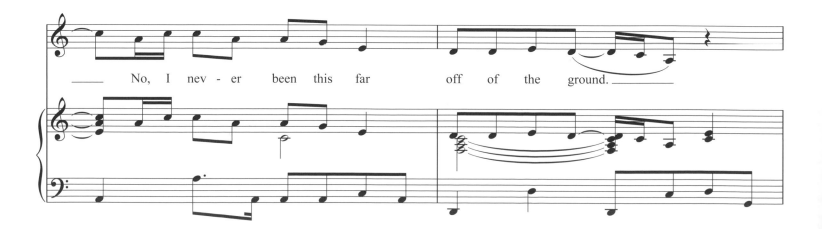

_____ No, I nev - er been this far off of the ground. _____

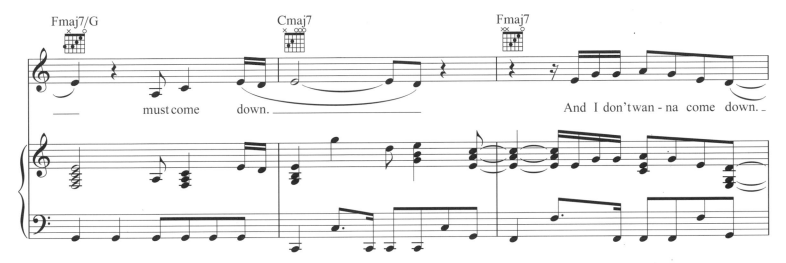

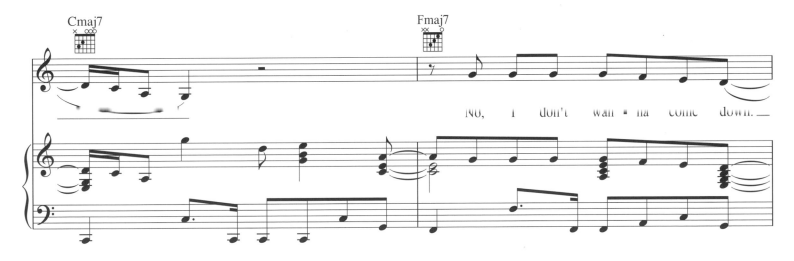

VELVET ELVIS

Words and Music by KACEY MUSGRAVES,
NATALIE HEMBY and LUKE DICK

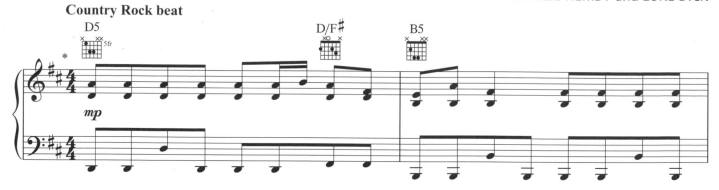

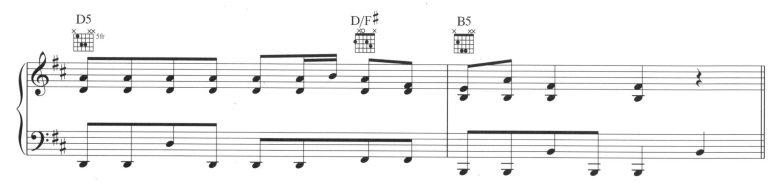

All I ev-er want-ed was some-thing clas - sic, the kind of

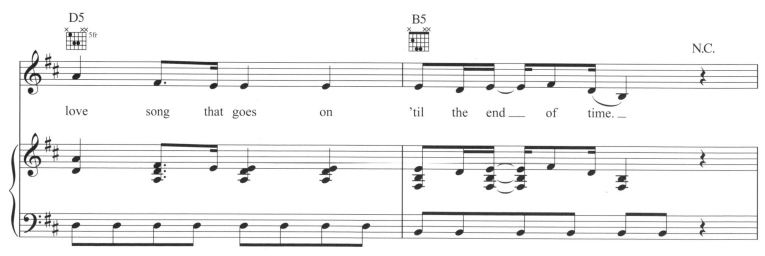

love song that goes on 'til the end __ of time. __

Recorded a half-step lower

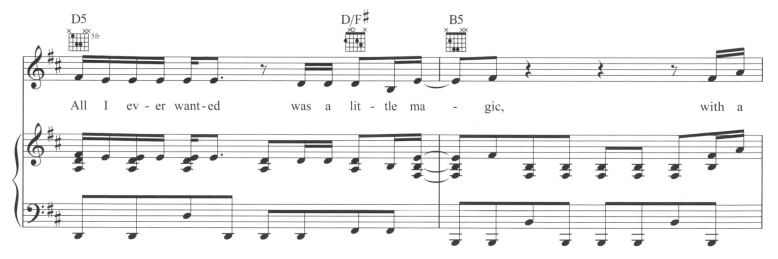

All I ev-er want-ed was a lit-tle ma - gic, with a

good laught, jet black spar-kle in ___ his eyes. ___ You're my vel - vet

El - vis, I ain't nev-er gon-na take you down. Mak-ing ev-'ry-bod-y

jeal - ous when they step in-to my house.

Soft to the touch, feels like love, knew it as soon as I felt it. You're __ my

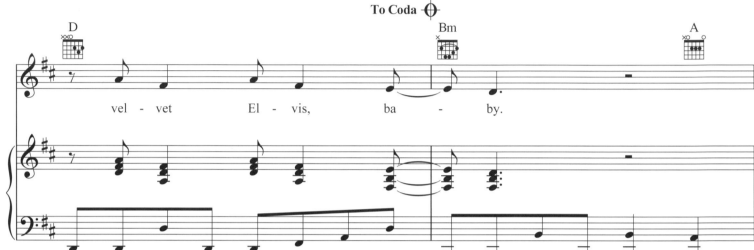

To Coda ⊕

vel - vet El - vis, ba - by.

I don't real - ly care 'bout the Mo - na Li - sa. I need a

Grace - land kind of man who's al - ways on ___ my mind. __ I want to

show you off ev - 'ry eve - ning. Go

out with you___ in pow - der blue___ and tease my hair___ up high. You're my vel - vet

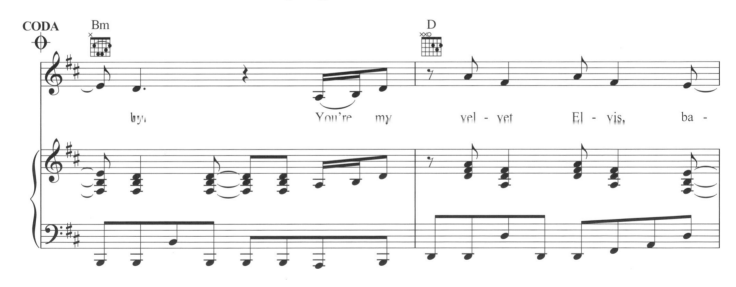

- by. You're my vel - vet El - vis, ba -

- by. I

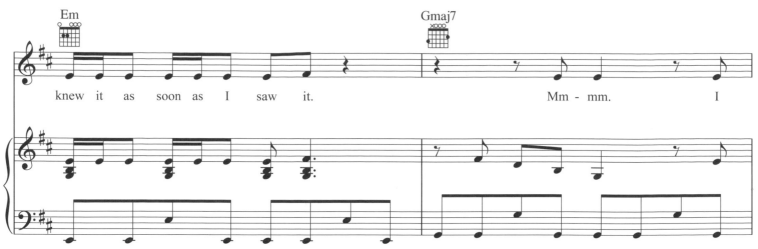

knew it as soon as I saw it. Mm - mm. I

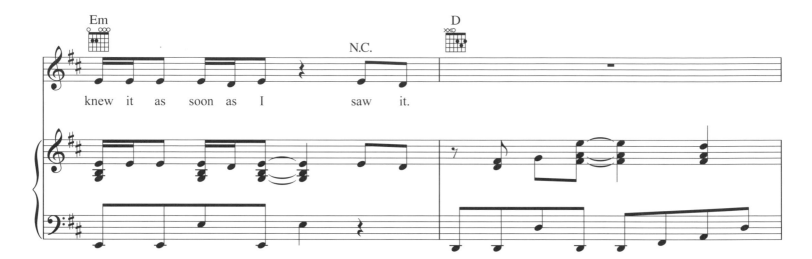

knew it as soon as I saw it.

Yeah. You're my vel - vet

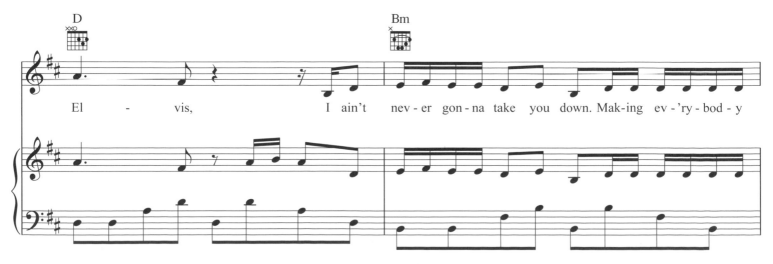

El - vis, I ain't nev - er gon - na take you down. Mak - ing ev - 'ry - bod - y

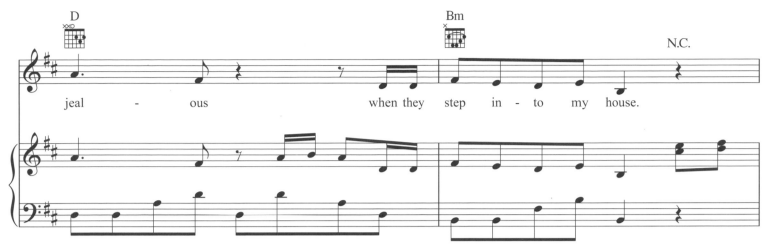

jeal - ous when they step in - to my house.

Soft to the touch, feels like love, knew it as soon as I felt it. You're my

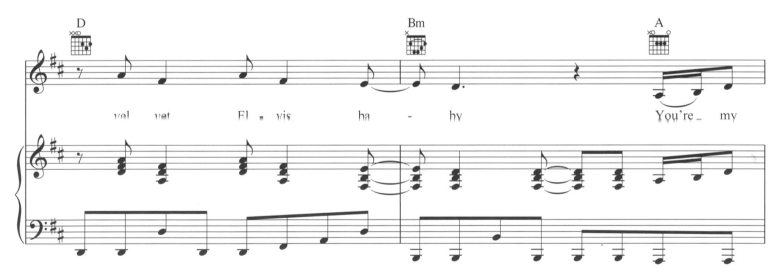

vel - vet El - vis ba - by You're my

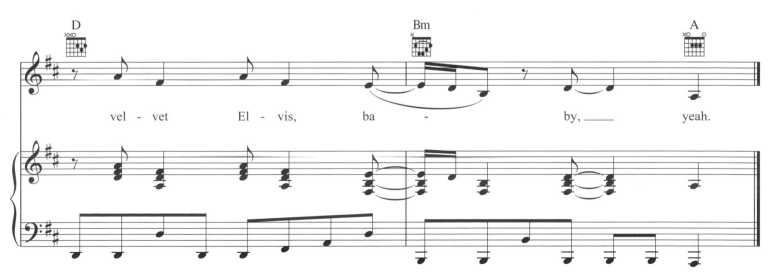

vel - vet El - vis, ba - by, yeah.

WONDER WOMAN

Words and Music by KACEY MUSGRAVES,
JESSE FRASURE, AMY WADGE
and HILLARY LINDSEY

* *Recorded a half step lower*

we're go - ing to. / I can
try - ing not to get hurt. / I know

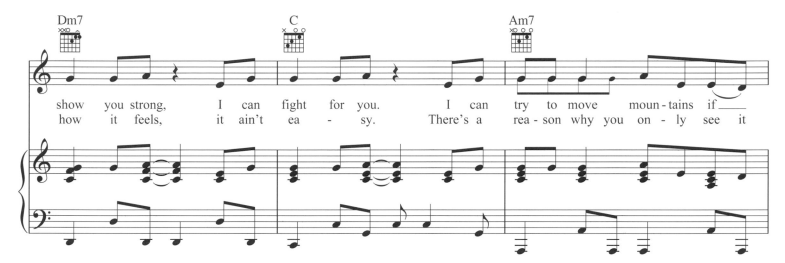

show you strong, I can fight for you. I can try to move moun-tains if ____
how it feels, it ain't ea - sy. There's a rea - son why you on - ly see it

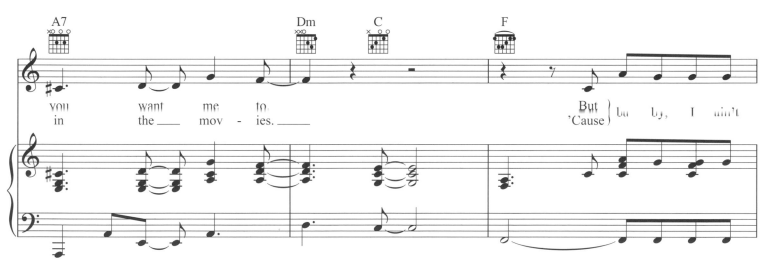

you want me to.
in the ____ mov - ies. ____

But
'Cause } ba - by, I ain't

Won - der Wom - an.

I don't know how to las - so the { love ____ / truth ____ } out of you.

You don't know how __ to fly, _____ no. ____ Mmm. _____

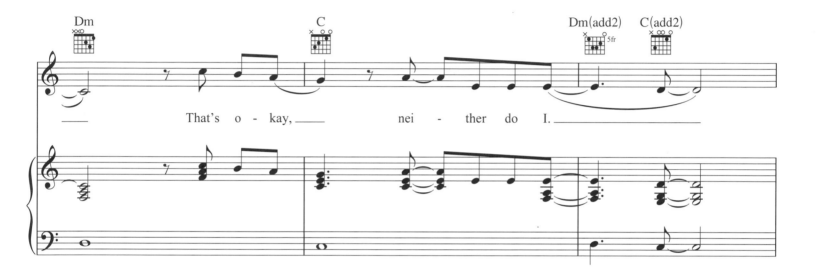

__ That's o - kay, ____ nei - ther do I. _____

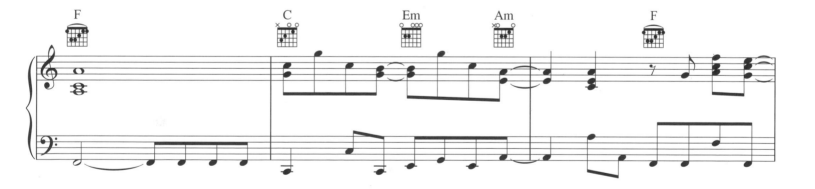

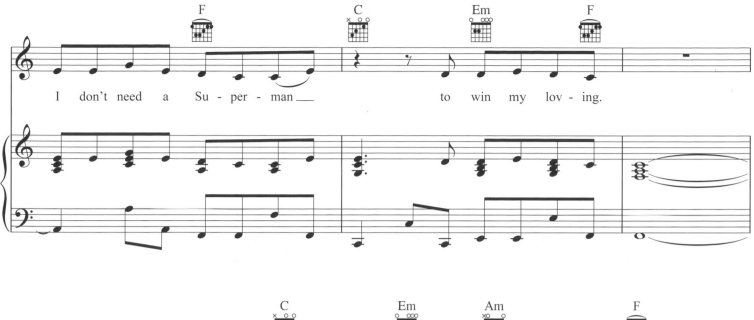

I don't need a Su-per-man ___ to win my lov-ing.

'Cause ba-by, I ain't Won-der Wom-an.

Yeah, I know I ain't Won-der Wom-an.

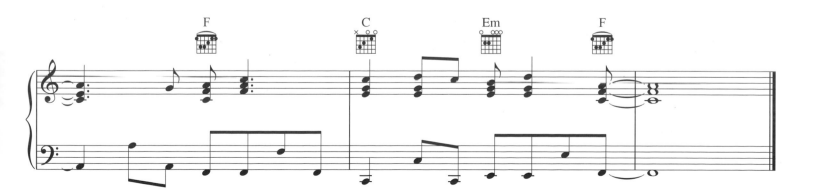

GOLDEN HOUR

Words and Music by KACEY MUSGRAVES,
IAN FITCHUK and DANIEL TASHIAN

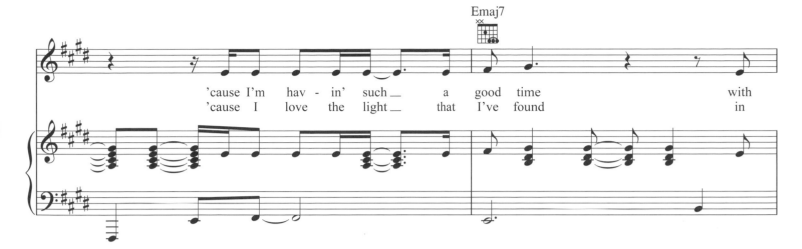

'cause I'm hav-in' such __ a good time with
'cause I love the light __ that I've found in

you.
you.

Ba - by, don't you know __

that you're my gold - en hour, _____

the col - or of my sky? _____

You've set my world on ____ fi - ____ re. ____

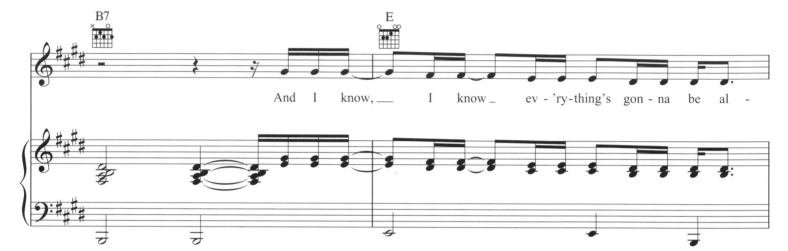

And I know, ____ I know ____ ev - 'ry-thing's gon - na be al -

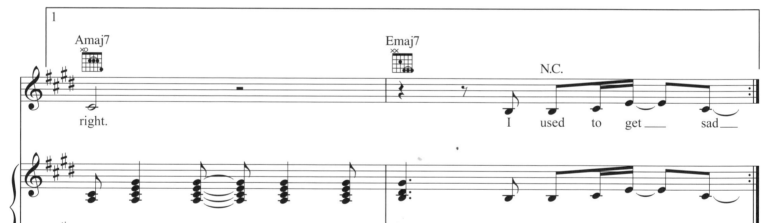

right. I used to get ____ sad ____

right, ____ mm. ____

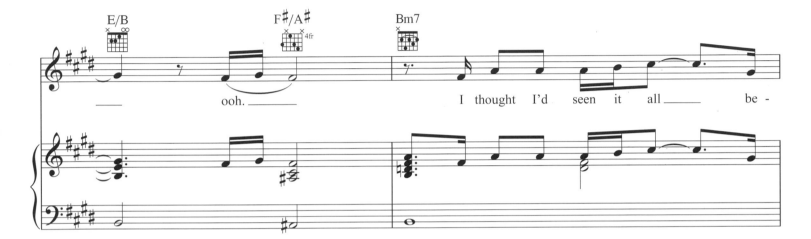

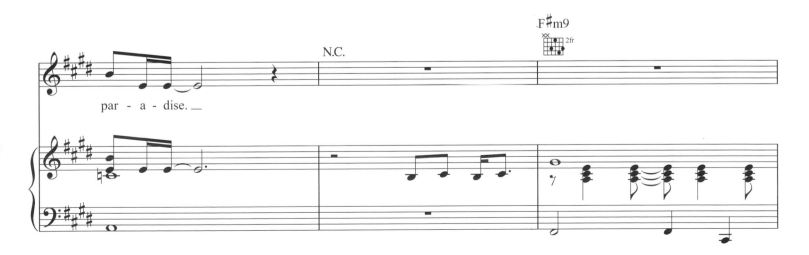

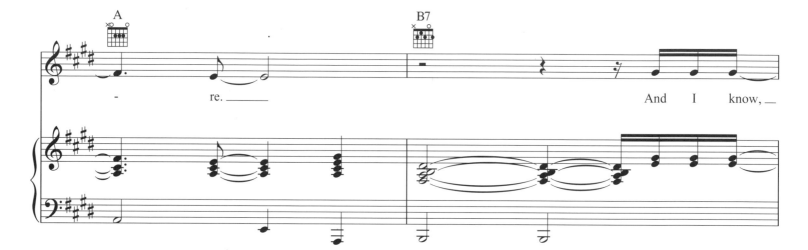

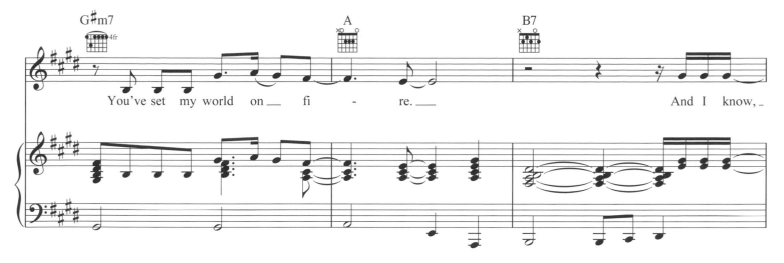

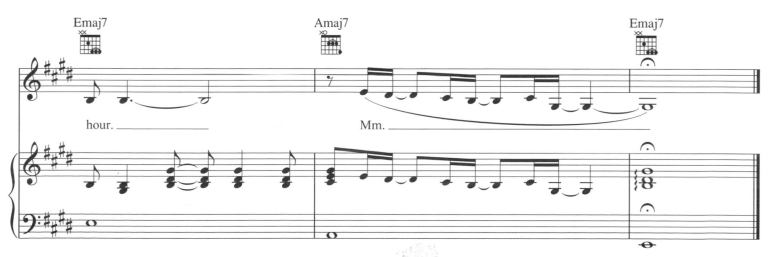

RAINBOW

Words and Music by KACEY MUSGRAVES,
SHANE McANALLY and NATALIE HEMBY

Piano Ballad

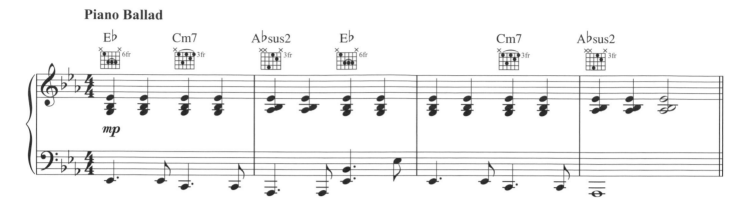

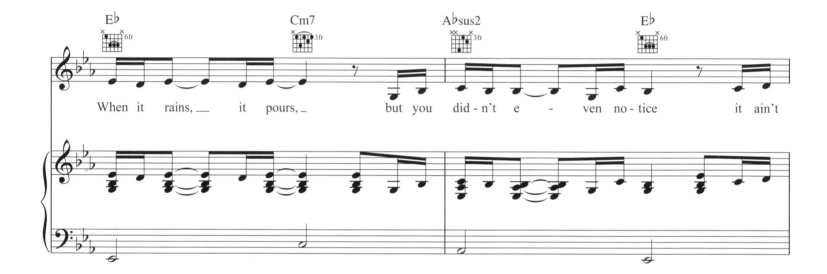

When it rains, __ it pours, __ but you did-n't e - ven no-tice it ain't

rain-ing an-y-more. __ It's hard to breathe when all __ you know is the

strug-gle of stay-ing ___ a - bove ___ the ris-ing wa - ter line. ___

Well, the sky has fi - n'lly o - pened, the

rain and wind stopped blow - ing, But you're stuck out ___ in the same ___ old storm a - gain. ___

You hold tight to your ___ um-brel - la. Well, dar - ling,

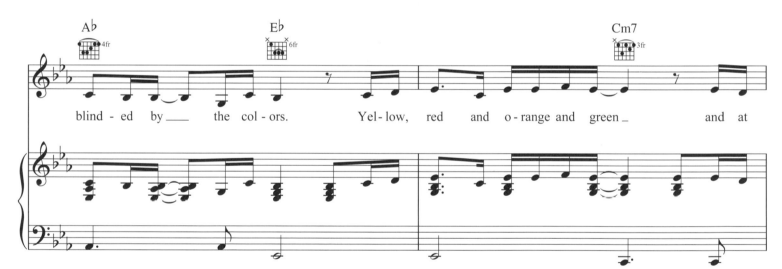

D.S. al Coda

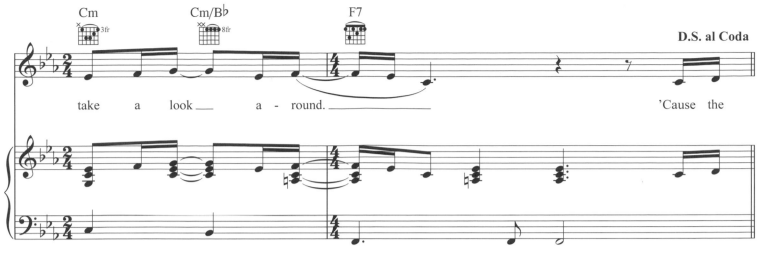

take a look ___ a - round. _____ 'Cause the

CODA

o - ver ___ your head. _____

Oh, tie

up the boat, ___ take off your coat ___ and take a look ___ a - round. ___

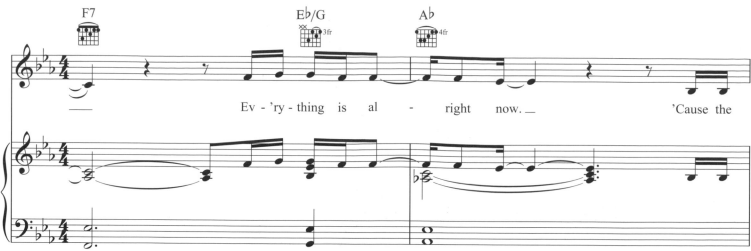

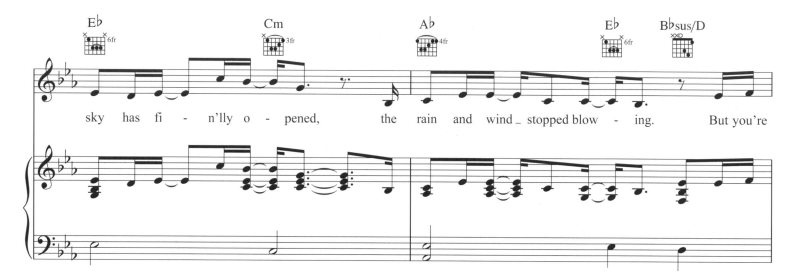

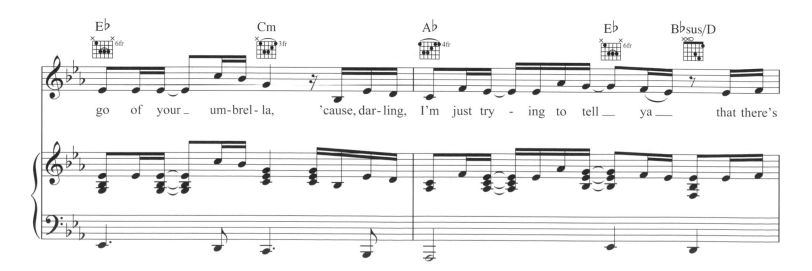

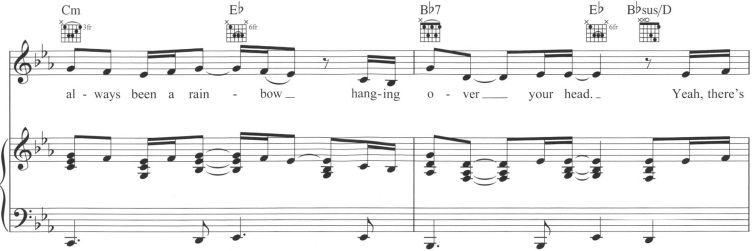

al - ways been a rain - bow __ hang-ing o - ver ___ your head. __ Yeah, there's

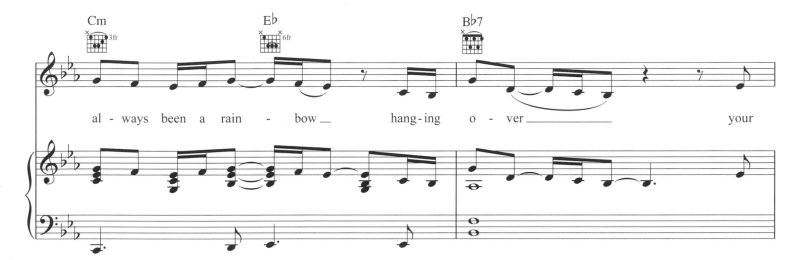

al - ways been a rain - bow __ hang-ing o - ver _____ your

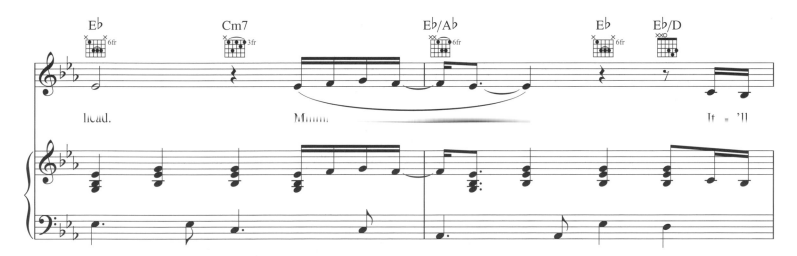

head. Mmm It - 'll

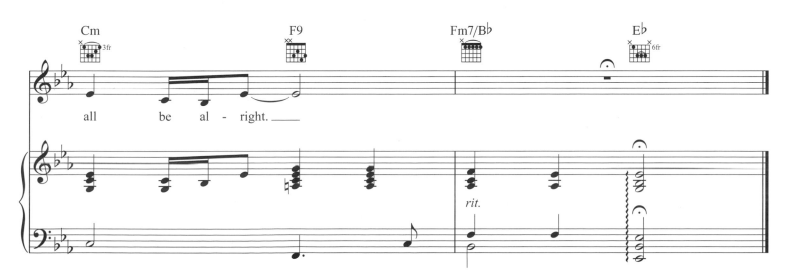

all be al - right. ___

MORE FROM YOUR FAVORITE ARTISTS

CAMILA CABELLO – CAMILA

All ten tracks from the 2018 debut album by this Fifth Harmony alum which debuted at the top of the Billboard® 200 album charts. Our folio includes piano/vocal/guitar arrangements for the hit single "Havana" plus: All These Years • Consequences • In the Dark • Inside Out • Into It • Never Be the Same • Real Friends • She Loves Control • Something's Gotta Give.
00268761 P/V/G......................................$17.99

ARIANA GRANDE – MY EVERYTHING

This sophomore solo effort from the Nickelodeon TV star turned R&B songstress reached #1 on the Billboard® 200 album charts and has produced several popular hits. A dozen tracks are featured in piano/vocal/guitar arrangements: Be My Baby • Best Mistake • Break Free • Break Your Heart Right Back • Hands on Me • Intro • Just a Little Bit of Your Heart • Love Me Harder • My Everything • One Last Time • Problem • Why Try.
00146042 P/V/G......................................$17.99

NIALL HORAN – FLICKER

This debut solo effort from One Direction's Niall Horan debuted at the top of the Billboard® 200 album charts. Our piano/vocal/guitar folio includes 13 songs from the album: Fire Away • Flicker • Mirrors • On My Own • On the Loose • Paper Houses • Seeing Blind • Since We're Alone • Slow Hands • This Town • The Tide • Too Much to Ask • You and Me.
00255614 P/V/G......................................$17.99

IMAGINE DRAGONS – EVOLVE

This 3rd studio album by Nevada rock band Imagine Dragons was released in the summer of 2017 and reached #2 on the Billboard® 200 album charts. Our matching folio includes piano, vocal & guitar arrangements to the singles "Believer" and "Thunder" as well as 9 moresongs: Dancing in the Dark • I Don't Know Why • I'll Make It Up to You • Mouth of the River • Rise Up • Start Over • Walking the Wire • Whatever It Takes • Yesterday.
00243903 P/V/G......................................$17.99

MAROON 5 – RED PILL BLUES

Maroon 5 keeps churning out the hits with their sixth studio album, this 2017 release led by the single "What Lovers Do" featuring Sza. Our songbooks features piano/vocal/guitar arrangements of this song and 14 more: Best 4 U • Bet My Heart • Closure • Cold • Denim Jacket • Don't Wanna Know • Girls like You • Help Me Out • Lips on You • Plastic Rose • Visions • Wait • Whiskey • Who I Am.
00261247 P/V/G......................................$17.99

P!NK – BEAUTIFUL TRAUMA

This 7th studio album from pop superstar Pink topped the Billboard® 200 album charts upon its release in 2017 led by the single "What About Us." Our matching folio features this song and a dozen more for piano, voice and guitar: Barbies • Beautiful Trauma • Better Life • But We Lost It • For Now • I Am Here • Revenge • Secrets • Whatever You Want • Where We Go • Wild Hearts Can't Be Broken • You Get My Love.
00255621 P/V/G......................................$17.99

ED SHEERAN – DIVIDE

This third studio album release from Ed Sheeran topped the Billboard® 200 album charts upon its March 2017 release, led by the singles "Castle on the Hill" and "Shape of You." Our matching folio includes these two hits, plus 14 others: Barcelona • Dive • Eraser • Galway Girl • Hearts Don't Break Around Here • New Man • Perfect • Save Myself • What Do I Know? • and more.
00233553 P/V/G......................................$17.99

SAM SMITH – THE THRILL OF IT ALL

Smith's sophomore album release in 2017 topped the Billboard® 200 album charts. This matching folio features 14 songs: Baby, You Make Me Crazy • Burning • Him • Midnight Train • No Peace • Nothing Left for You • One Day at a Time • One Last Song • Palace • Pray • Say It First • Scars • The Thrill of It All • Too Good at Goodbyes.
00257746 P/V/G......................................$19.99

TAYLOR SWIFT – REPUTATION

Taylor's 2017 album release continues her chart-topping success, debuting on the Billboard® 200 chart at number 1, led by the first singles "Look What You Made Me Do" and "...Ready for It." Our songbook features these 2 songs plus 13 more arranged for piano and voice with guitar chord frames: Call It What You Want • Dancing with Our Hands Tied • Delicate • Don't Blame Me • Dress • End Game • Getaway Car • Gorgeous • I Did Something Bad • King of My Heart • New Year's Day • So It Goes... • This Is Why We Can't Have Nice Things.
00262694 P/V/G......................................$17.99

HAL•LEONARD®

Contents, prices, and availability subject to change without notice.

For a complete listing of the products we have available, visit us online at **www.halleonard.com**